Brilliant Class-led Assemblies

for Key Stage 2

Effective, Flexible and Fun Curriculum-based Assemblies

Katie Harris and Amanda MacNaughton

Brilliant Publications

Publisher's information

Brilliant Publications
www.brilliantpublications.co.uk

Sales Office
BEBC (Brilliant Publications)
Albion Close, Parkstone, Poole, Dorset BH12 3LL UK
Tel: 01202 712910   Fax: 0845 1309300
e-mail: brilliant@bebc.co.uk

Editorial Office
Unit 10, Sparrow Hall Farm
Edlesborough
Dunstable Bedfordshire LU6 2ES UK
Tel: 01525 222292   Fax: 01525 222720
e-mail: info@brilliantpublications.co.uk

The name 'Brilliant Publications' and the logo are registered trade marks.

Written by Katie Harris and Amanda MacNaughton.
Cover illustration and inside illustrations by Jamie Smith

© Katie Harris and Amanda MacNaughton
ISBN 978-1-905780-14-3

First printed in the UK in 2007 by Lightning Source
10   9   8   7   6   5   4   3   2   1

If you would like further information on any of our other titles or to request a catalogue, please look at our website www.brilliantpublications.co.uk or telephone 01525 222292.

Contents

Introduction

What is the purpose of this book?

As teachers, we know that time is a precious commodity and that there are always other pressing deadlines to meet when it's your turn for the 'dreaded class assembly'! Our aim is to provide effective, stress-free, curriculum-based assemblies, all of which have been tried and tested.

How can these assemblies work for you?

Select an assembly, collect your resources and off you go! It really is as simple as that. However, as practising teachers, we realize that no class is the same and so these assemblies are designed to be flexible. Your assembly can become as elaborate as you wish or as straight-forward as you have the time or energy for! We know from experience that all the assemblies in this book can be introduced and executed within one week – they are not intended to be complicated productions that take up valuable time.

These assemblies can be used to consolidate previous learning
or
to inform your medium-term planning.

Helpful hints

- Tailor your assembly to suit your needs, for example by simply changing the number of roles needed, by having fewer large speaking parts, by giving each pupil a little more to say or even by adapting the props and costumes.
- Background work can be included, changed or omitted depending on work covered in class and stage of the term in which assembly is performed.
- Children who don't want a speaking part can always be involved with sound, props etc.
- Stage directions can be adapted according to space available.
- Where there are empty brackets (...............), this is an indication that other information needs to be inserted, for example a name or a place.
- Depending on the ability and age of the children, these scripts could be learned or read.
- Many classes of varying backgrounds, abilities and ages have successfully performed these assemblies, so go on, give one a go!

For some of the assemblies, signs are needed for pupils to hold up or have attached to them in some way. To save you time, all the signs required can be downloaded from the following page on our website: www.brilliantpublications.co.uk/1014_signs.pdf

Away with the Pharaohs

Subject:	History
Area of Study:	Ancient Egypt
Summary:	Two children struggle with their history homework until they are magically transported back to the age of the Pharaohs. Vivid images and captivating verse bring Ancient Egypt alive and provide our two friends with the inspiration they need.
Timing:	20 minutes approx
Props:	• large scrapbook, titled 'Ancient Egypt' • large fans • long piece of blue material • sunhats • sunglasses • boxes disguised as large stones with rope attached • pretend jugs, goblets and baskets of food
Music:	Magical-sounding instrumental music
Background Work:	• Non-fiction writing about the River Nile and about how the pyramids were built (www.interoz.com/egypt/kids/History.htm) • Dancing/miming of athletics – wrestling, javelin throwing etc • Poems written about the Pharaohs

Cast and costumes:

Part	No. needed	Suggested costumes
Narrators	4	School uniform/clothing
Cleo	1	Jeans, t-shirt, trainers, sunglasses, sunhat
Tony	1	Jeans, shirt, trainers, sunglasses, sunhat
River Nile	6 (lined up in 2s)	All in blue, carrying blue material over their heads
Mr Khamun	1	Trousers, shirt and tie
Slaves	4	White sheets wrapped in toga style with belts, sandals or bare feet
Servant	1	As slaves
Pharaoh	1	White sheets wrapped in toga style, coloured sash, eye make-up
Pharaoh's wife	1	As pharaoh above
Chief Advisor/Priests/Scribes	4–6	Those who play the parts of slaves pulling stones can also be priests, scribes
Fan Bearers	2	As slaves
Athletes	4	White shorts and t-shirt
Mummies	2	All in white, head and ankles wrapped in bandages

Suggested Script – Away with the Pharaohs

Narrator 1   Welcome to our assembly. We have been learning about the Ancient Egyptians and would like to share some of our learning with you.

Tony and Cleo are lying around looking bored, confused and fed up. Their Ancient Egypt book is lying on the floor near them.

Narrator 1   Have you ever been at a loss for words when it comes to writing your homework? Yes? Well, that's exactly how we find our friends Tony and Cleo. They're struggling to remember anything Mr Khamun's taught them all term about the Ancient Egyptians!

Mr Khamun walks across stage muttering about 'children of today' and how they should listen more carefully etc ...

Cleo   A day in Ancient Egypt ... homework ... I hate it!

Tony   (*Picking up book and opening it.*) Me too; I haven't got a clue what to write!

Cleo   What about this picture of the River Nile
– surely we can use that in some way? (*Pointing to picture in book.*)

Tony   Did you know the River Nile is over 4 000 miles long? (*Music starts playing.*) It flows from ... hang on a minute. Can you hear that? It sounds like music and it's getting louder!

Cleo   Oooooooh! Wooooah! I think I'm getting sucked into the book!

Tony/Cleo   HELP!

The music continues as Tony and Cleo wake up, completely awestruck with what they see – the River Nile!

Cleo   Wh ... wh ... where are we? Have we ... ?

Tony   I think we have – we're really in Ancient Egypt - and that really is the River Nile!

Brilliant Publications

The River Nile moves down the centre aisle and around the stage, each pair of children moving up and down simultaneously to give the impression of the river rippling.

River Nile   We are the River Nile
We are the River Nile
We travel from our source
We travel on a course
For over 4 000 miles
We ripple and we roar
Stop to rest for a while
A river with great style
Oh! The great River Nile.
(Repeat before settling on the ground.)

Cleo   It's just like I imagined it would be! Do you remember Mr Khamun saying he thought it was probably the most amazing river in the world? Well, I think he was right!

Mr Khamun   *(Reads pupil's non-fiction writing about the River Nile.)*

Narrator 2   The children begin to wander around in the blazing sun to see what else they might find. In the distance, they can hear people coming.

Tony   Wooooh! It's so-o-o hot! Those temperature graphs we made with Miss Thermo on the computer are more accurate than I thought!

Cleo   It's boiling – I wish I had my shorts on! Lucky for us we had our sunhats and sunglasses in our pockets! I can hear people coming – quick! Hide!

They jump back as the slaves enter, dragging stones by their ropes and chanting. Alternatively, children can take a line each from each verse.

Slaves   We've hauled a hundred rocks today
We've pulled a thousand blocks today
We've walked a million miles today
No more for now, we all do pray.

We take a limestone rock
We cut a limestone block
We do the pyramid stamp
We roll it up that ramp.

We're heaving on these ropes
Until we reach the top
And when the sun goes down
We do the pyramid stop!

© Katie Harris and Amanda MacNaughton   **Brilliant Publications**

Slaves drag stones to one side of stage and drop the ropes. They repeat the chant, this time with hand moves (can be choreographed by the children).

Cleo   I'd hate to have their job, wouldn't you? And in this heat, too!
              – I'm just tired from watching them!

Tony   All that work, just for one pyramid – I can't believe it!

Cleo   Yes, don't you remember that writing about the pyramid we had to do at school? Mr Khamun said it took about 20 years and hundreds of thousands of people to build the Great Pyramid at Gizza.

Mr Khamun *(Reads pupil's non-fiction writing about how a pyramid was built and who was involved.)*

Whilst non-fiction writing is being read out, Tony and Cleo continue wandering. They find a door and decide to go through; they find themselves in the Pharaoh's court.

Tony   Let's go through here- this is the most amazing experience I've ever had - it even beats my latest computer game.

Cleo   Me too … oh wow!

Servant   Sssshhh! Kneel down now!

Narrator 3 Not knowing where they were going, Tony and Cleo have accidentally stumbled into the Pharaoh's court where slaves, priests and scribes gather to worship and entertain the Pharaoh and his wife.

Court of the Pharaoh – Pharaoh and his wife sitting on thrones, fan bearers either side, slaves serving food and wine.

Chief Advisor SLAVES! Serve the wine *(clap, clap)*.

Servants serve the Pharaoh first, then his wife, followed by any others.

Chief Advisor ATHLETES! You are now called upon to entertain your Pharaoh with your amazing athletic skills *(clap, clap)*.

The athletes line up ready but one forgets to bow.

Chief Advisor How dare you show such insolence to your Pharaoh! Bow to him now! Get on your knees! Kiss the ground before his Royal Highness! (*Turning to the Pharaoh*) Pharaoh, I apologize – would you care for this man to be tortured?

Pharaoh nods and points towards outside. The man is taken away by one of the servants to be beaten – cries are heard when he has left the room.

Chief Advisor ATHLETES! You may perform! (*clap, clap*)

Athletes perform their duties – the wrestlers mime wrestling, the javelin is thrown. There is polite clapping. Before leaving, the athletes bow once more.

Chief Advisor (*To the athletes*) You may leave (*clap, clap*).

Tony Quick! I want to leave before we get seen by the Pharaoh ... we'd get beaten for sure!

Cleo I know. We'll have to be careful though – let's go.

Court clears the stage and the two children are left alone.

Cleo Phew ... ! That was horrible, just like on our Egyptian day we had at school. The Pharaoh was so frightening.

Tony No he wasn't! They do have the best lives, though! Remember those poems we had to write at school?

Mr Khamun (*Reads a selected number of poems written about the Pharaohs and their lives.*)

Whilst the poem(s) are being read, a white sheet is placed over the stones left by the slaves and the mummies discreetly hide behind them.

Cleo (*Nodding to the stones and whispering.*) What do you think's under there?

Tony Only one way to find out!

He lifts off the cover and up jump the mummies.

Mummies	For so many years we've been soundly asleep In a pyramid tomb in a coma so deep Not a drop did we drink, not a morsel to eat Now our bandages sag and we're feeling the heat We have no clothes to wear, we're so terribly thin We've lost all our curves and we're down to one chin Hear that rumbling, grumbling noise from our tummies? Give us food! Give us food! We are such hungry mummies!

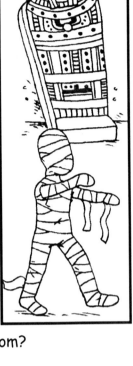

Cleo   Oh! Sorry, all I've got are these (...........................) (*pulls some kind of food from her pocket*). Will these do?

Mummies   Mmmm ...

Magical-sounding instrumental music begins.

Tony   Cleo, can you hear that music again? Where's it coming from?

Cleo   I don't know, but I feel all weird again. Aaggh ... ! What's happening?

As the music plays, the children are again being transported in time – they arrive back at Tony's looking at the Ancient Egypt book.

Tony   Wow! That was wicked - I know exactly what I'm going to write for my homework now! Let's get started!

Cleo   Me too – we'll show that Mr Khamun what we're really made of!

Narrator 4   Thank you for watching our assembly. We hope you have enjoyed it!

Henry and All Those Wives!

Subject: History

Area of Study: The Tudors

Summary: A focus on King Henry VIII is bound to entertain children and yet cause them to question his antics. This assembly takes a somewhat light-hearted view of King Henry's reign, allowing the audience to form their own opinion on this controversial monarch.

Timing: 20–25 minutes approx

Props:
- 2 chairs dressed as a throne ● axe ● baby doll
- signs: '3 years later', '1 year later', '6 months later', 'Divorced' 'In the same month!', '7 months later', '2 years later', 'Catherine Parr' and '4 years later'

Music: Tudor-style music

Background Work:
- Framed Tudor portraits
- Class survey – King Henry VIII: a good or bad King?
- 'If I were King/Queen, I would ... '

Cast and costumes:

Part	No needed	Suggested costumes
Narrators	6	School uniform/clothing
King Henry VIII	1	Trousers, white frilly shirt, velvet cape, cushioned stomach, beard, crown
Pope	1	Mitre hat, long red robe, gold stole, crook
Catherine of Aragon	1	Long dresses – long sleeves, hair up if possible, half coronet with short, attached back veil
Anne Boleyn	1	
Jane Seymour	1	
Anne of Cleves	1	
Catherine Howard	1	
Catherine Parr	1	
Servant	1	3/4-length trousers, white shirt
Executioner	1	All in black, black eye mask, axe
Mary (non-speaking)	1	As wives, without veil
Elizabeth (non-speaking)	1	As wives, without veil
Hans Holbein & Artists	Remaining children	Big white shirt, trousers, beret, moustache

Suggested Script – Henry and All Those Wives!

Narrator 1   Welcome to our assembly. We have been learning about King Henry VIII and deciding whether we think he was a good or bad king.

King Henry and his first wife, Catherine of Aragon, sit on the thrones; Mary sits at their feet.

Henry   Catherine, we have one daughter, Mary. Correct?

Catherine   Yes, Henry.

Henry   Well, I want a son! You're clearly not good enough for me if you can't provide me with a son. You'll have to go!

Catherine   Yes, Henry. (*Catherine gets up and leaves.*)

Henry   (*Snaps his fingers and the servant comes running.*) (*To servant*) Send a message to the Pope immediately, saying I wish to divorce her!

Servant   Immediately, Your Majesty! (*Runs off towards the Pope as he enters.*) Good day to you, Pope, sir (*bowing*). Henry Tudor, King of England, wishes to divorce his wife, sir.

Pope   Hmmmmm ... this is not something I approve of, but I don't really want to upset that man ... hmmmmmm ... . I'd best not say anything at all. Hopefully he'll change his mind!

Servant   (*Comes back to Henry.*) The Pope is not happy, Your Majesty. He does not approve!

Henry   Really? Well, I don't want to be part of HIS Church, then. I'll make one of my own! Hmmm ... the Church of England, that's what I'll call it. Now, it will need a good leader... aaah ... ME of course! (*Anne Boleyn walks past.*) Ooooh, hello-o there, you beautiful woman! Who are you?

Anne   Anne Boleyn, Your Majesty.

Henry   Well, come here, my dear (*patting the empty throne*). Would you like to be my wife? Yes! (*giving her no time to answer.*) Wonderful – that's settled then!

Narrator 2 Goodness. What a heartless man! Wife number 1 dropped like a hotcake. Wife number 2 grabbed off the street!

Narrator 3 Give the poor man a break – it was vital he had a son to continue the Tudor name.

Child walks across stage with a sign saying '3 years later'. Henry and Anne sit on their thrones; Elizabeth and Mary sit at their feet.

Henry Anne, we have one daughter, Elizabeth. Correct?

Anne Yes, Henry.

Henry Well, I want a son! You're clearly not good enough for me if you can't provide me with a son. You'll have to go!

Anne Yes, Henry.

Henry Executioner. Chop off her head!

Executioner (*Looking excited.*) Immediately Your Majesty! (*Takes Anne Boleyn away, looking at her hair.*) Just a little off the top then, dear? (*Anne sobs.*)

Henry Jane! Jane! The coast is clear – come to me, my dear!

Jane (*Comes running to sit on the empty throne.*) Oh, Henry - at last!

Narrator 2 This man is unbelievable – wife number 2 provides him with a second beautiful daughter and he demands her head on a block!

Narrator 3 The man wants a son! Let's see how wife number 3 fares!

Child walks across stage with a sign saying '1 year later'. Henry sits on his throne cradling a baby, and Mary and Elizabeth sit at his feet.

Henry At last I have a son! We shall call him Edward and he shall …

Servant I'm sorry, sir, but your wife didn't make it. I'm afraid she died this morning.

Henry Oh … oh dear (*Looking and sounding very sad*).

Narrator 2 (*Blowing nose loudly into handkerchief.*) Oh, how very sad – poor Jane!

Narrator 3   Agreed. But at least Henry now has his son. Something tells me, however, that he might still be on the hunt for a new wife. (*Narrator 2 looks shocked.*)

Child walks across stage with a sign saying '3 years later'.

Henry   (*Looking at a picture of Anne of Cleves.*) Well, I suppose she'll do. Bring her in!

Anne of Cleves enters (unattractive, protruding teeth, ungainly walk). Henry looks appalled.

Henry   Oh! How awful! They were supposed to send me (*looking at the picture*) a beautiful woman, not this horse-like creature. (*Tosses the picture over his head.*) Servant – send a message to Hans and his gang, will you? I demand a jolly good portrait.

Servant   Immediately, Your Majesty!

Hans Holbein and other artists enter carrying paintbrushes and other materials. They begin painting Henry and his children. Tudor-style music plays whilst Henry shouts demands.

Henry   Paint my best side – difficult to choose, I know! Let me see, let me see … mmm … lose that chin, will you?

Artists gradually turn around to face the audience and show their finished Tudor-style portraits.

Child walks across stage with a sign saying '6 months later'. Anne of Cleves walks off stage with a sign round her neck saying 'Divorced'.

Henry   (*Dusting off his hands.*) Well that took care of her … NEXT!

Child walks across stage with a sign saying 'In the same month!'

Henry   Catherine! Catherine! The coast is clear!

Catherine   Oh, Henry – at last!

Child walks across stage with a sign saying '7 months later'.

Henry   Catherine – you have given me no sons and no happiness – you'll have to go! EXECUTIONER! Chop off her head!

| **Executioner** | Immediately, Your Majesty! (*Takes Catherine Howard away.*) At least he'll no longer be a pain in the neck for you, my dear! (*Catherine sobs.*) |

Narrator 2   (*Shaking his/her head.*) This man has no mercy! No feelings, in fact!

Narrator 3   That's not true; he just wasn't willing to lie about his feelings – he knew what he wanted!

Child walks across stage with a sign saying '2 years later'.

Catherine Parr walks past Henry with a sign on her saying 'Catherine Parr'.

Henry   Ooh, hello. I rather like the name Catherine – do you want to get married? Yes, wonderful! (*Giving her no time to answer.*)

Child walks across stage with a sign saying '4 years later'.

Servant   I'm sorry, m'lady, but King Henry has died! You'll have to leave as you're no longer needed!

Catherine looks sad.

Although you DID survive!

Narrator 2   (*Counting with his/her fingers from 1 to 6, stating what happened to each wife each time*) DIVORCED ... BEHEADED ... DIED ... DIVORCED ... BEHEADED ... SURVIVED!

Narrator 3   He certainly had a busy life as King!

Narrator 4   After researching Henry's life and time as King, we carried out a vote. These were the results:
(......) people thought Henry VIII was a GOOD King.
(......) people couldn't decide whether he was a good or bad King.
A majority/minority (delete as appropriate) of (......) people thought, however, that Henry VIII was a bad King! I wonder what you think.

Narrator 5   We thought about what we would do and what changes we might make if we were King or Queen.

Everyone   If I were King/Queen, I would ... .

Narrator 6   Thank you for listening to our assembly. We hope you have enjoyed sharing our work with us!

We'll Meet Again

Subject: History

Area of Study: World War II

Summary: An assembly that brings home the reality of evacuation during the Second World War. Children will experience the highs and the lows that evacuation brought through drama, music and literacy.

Timing: 25 minutes approx

Props:
- Map of Europe with countries highlighted which were involved in WWII ● sweets ● bacon ● eggs ● milk ● sugar ● butter ● cheese

Music: *Quartermaster's Stores* (www.scoutsongs.com/lyrics/quartermasters.html), *We'll Meet Again* (ingeb.org/songs/wellmeet.html); sound effects; siren

Background Work:
- A range of creative writing based around the theme of evacuation, including poems, quotes, letters home etc.
- Gas masks made from card
- Gas mask holders
- Identification labels

Cast and costumes:

Part	No needed	Suggested costumes
Narrators	10	School uniform clothing
Know it alls (KIAs)	4	School uniform clothing
Silly	1	Same as evacuees
Spotty	1	Same as evacuees
Smelly	1	Same as evacuees
Decent	1	Same as evacuees
Evacuees	Rest of class	Evacuee costume: Provide children with photographs of evacuees to inspire home-made costumes, ie shorts, white shirt, jacket and cap for boys; blouse, pinafore, thick winter coat and a bow in their hair for girls. (Keep it simple!)
Warden	1	Trousers, jacket, shirt, some kind of helmet
Billeting Officer (Mrs Perkins)	1	Dark-coloured formal dress, sensible shoes and coat
Nasty Lady	1	Slightly garish clothes suggesting air of importance
Nice Lady	1	Formal dress, sensible shoes, handbag
Nice Man	1	Suit

 Brilliant Publications

Suggested Script – We'll Meet Again

Narrator 1   Welcome to our assembly. We have been studying World War II this half-term, and so we aim to entertain you with our facts, plays and songs.

KIA 1   Did you know that … (*holding map*) the war began because Hitler, the German leader, wanted HIS country to be the most powerful in all of Europe? When Germany invaded Poland, Britain and France declared war on Germany.

KIA 2   Did you know that at the start of the war, many children were moved from the cities to safer areas in the countryside? This was called evacuation.

Evacuee   Children were assembled by their teachers at railway stations. When a child was evacuated, they had to wear a label (*all show labels*) and carry a gas mask in a holder (*all show gas masks and holders*).

Narrator 2   We have been thinking about what it would have been like to be evacuated, the experiences some children would have had and how they would have felt.

Narrator 3   We wrote letters 'home' as if we were those evacuees and poems about evacuation experiences.

A number of children could read out letters, poems or quotes they have written.

KIA 3   (*Children hold out food items as they mentioned*) Did you know that … food was rationed during the war? This was because there wasn't much food to go around and so it had to be shared out equally. Some foods that were rationed were …
        bacon
        milk
        butter
        cheese
        eggs
        sugar

Children   And sweets!

Narrator 4   During the war, one of the things people did to keep themselves happy and occupied was to sing songs. This song is called 'The Quartermaster's Stores'.

Everybody   (*Sing 'The Quartermaster's Stores'.*)

Narrator 5   We tried changing the words to some of the verses. These are some of our own ideas:

Group 1   (*Sing your song.*)

Group 2   (*Sing your song.*)

KIA 4   Did you know that ... when the air-raid siren sounded, meaning that the German bombers were on their way (*siren sounds – everyone runs to shelter behind benches*), everybody had to rush to an air-raid shelter? There were wardens on patrol who would do their best to encourage everyone to find shelter.

Warden   (*Speaking to KIA 4*) Move along please – nearest shelter this way!

Narrator 6   We imagined what it would have been like to be in an Anderson shelter for many hours, listening to the bombs dropping outside:

A couple of children could read out their accounts.

Narrator 7   We will now perform a short play to show how evacuation could be good or bad!

Enter 2 boys and 2 girls onto stage with a billeting officer.

Mrs Perkins   Come along now, children. We'll soon find new homes for you all. Stand up straight, dears. (*Children stand smartly.*) Flatten your hair – all of you - you look like you've come through a hedge backwards. (*Children flatten their hair.*)

Silly   I feel sick after that train journey, Miss.

Spotty   I miss my Mum. I hope we won't have to stay in the countryside for long.

Decent   Come on, everybody! This is really exciting. It's not every day that you get to move house!

Smelly   Yeh, and I bet our new Mums and Dads are going to be great!

Mrs Perkins   Well – look your best, my dears, because some of your foster families are coming right now.

Enter Nasty Lady, while a man and his wife wait at the side with their arms linked.

Nasty Lady   Good day to you, Mrs Perkins. Bit of a rum bunch you've got here today. These children from the slums of London, are they?

Mrs Perkins   Yes, but they're lovely children and very well behaved.

Nasty Lady   (*Sarcastically.*) I'm sure. Now this one won't do – he's too smelly! And this one is too silly! I can just tell by looking at her. And this one is far too spotty! I think it will have to be this child. She seems like the only decent one.

Decent   But I can't go with you on me own, Mrs. Me Ma and Pa said I had to stay wiv me bruvver and sister. We can't be split up!

Mrs Perkins   It does seem unfair, don't you think?

Nasty Lady   Not really! Well, I suppose it'll have to be this spotty one then. Come on, lad. You're coming home with me.

Nasty Lady pulls another child off by tugging his ear.

Narrator 8   Unfortunately, that child didn't have much fun when he was evacuated. Let's hope it's different for these brothers and sisters.

Smelly   I'm glad she's gone. I really didn't like the sound of her … I don't smell, do I?

Silly   Course you don't! Look – there's a man and a woman coming over.

Man and lady enter.

Man   Good afternoon, Mrs Perkins. What a lovely day it is today.

Lady   Look at these poor children. They must feel so strange and lonely, having to move away from their parents.

B Officer   (*Nods.*) It is a hard time for them, Miss. Can you take 3 of them back with you?

Lady   Oh my goodness! We came to help one child, maybe 2, but asking us to house 3 is preposterous. We haven't the room!

B Officer   It's just that they're all from the same family, you see.

Man   Come now, dear. Surely we can turn the attic into a bedroom. I can't bear to separate them. There!

Decent   Oh, please, Miss. We'll be ever so good and help you round the house and everything. And sometimes we'll be so quiet that you'll forget we're there.

Lady   (*Smiling.*) I can see that it's going to be difficult to say no to you. Well … we'd love to have you!

B Officer   You'll not regret this. They're a nice bunch. They'll give you lots of happiness.

Man   Come on, then, time to visit your new home. I hope you like cows, horses, pigs and chickens. We live on a farm.

Silly   A what? What's a pig, sir?

Smelly   I've read about pigs. Really smelly animals!

Decent   (*Laughing*) You'll fit right in, then!

All walk off together.

Narrator 9   So you can see that some children found lovely homes when they were evacuated. Some didn't even want to go back home when the war ended! As you can imagine, most families couldn't wait to be together again and that leads us into our next song: *'We'll Meet Again'.*

Everybody   (*Sing 'We'll Meet Again'.*)

Narrator 10   Thank you for coming to our assembly – we hope you have enjoyed it!

All Change!

Subject: Science

Area of Study: Reversible and irreversible changes

Summary: Year 6 revision for SATs can be boring, but this assembly brings reversible and irreversible changes to life! The science team (overseen by their bossy leader) help a group of pupils get to grips with changing materials .

Timing: 20 minutes approx

Props:
- OHP/whiteboard
- toy phone
- plates of pretend eggs, sausages and bread, both raw and cooked
- signs: 'SATS in Progress', 'Irreversible change', 'S', 'O', 'L', 'I' and 'D'

Music: None needed

Background Work:
- Knowledge of reversible and irreversible changes

Cast and costumes:

Part	No needed	Suggested costume
Narrators	6	School uniform/clothing
Pupil	1	School uniform/clothing
Leader of Science team	1	School uniform/clothing – he/she is never seen as they are sat on a chair facing away from the audience (like a James Bond villain). An echo tube/microphone would be useful to project their voice
Science team (ST)	5	Stereotypical scientists' uniform – white coat etc
Irreversible team (IRT)	5	School uniform/clothing
Reversible team (RT)	4	School uniform/clothing, but on back to front as much as possible
Particles	6	PE kit with red netball bibs

Suggested Script – All Change!

Narrator 1   In May, Year 6s have to take their Key Stage 2 National Tests.

Narrator 2   We've put together this assembly to make our revision in science exciting, to let you know what we've been doing and to help us remember it for ourselves!

Child seated as doing his/her SATs. Sign that says 'SATs in progress' over head.

Pupil   (*Holding the sheet, reads the question*) 'Explain what is meant by the process CHANGES OF STATE, showing the differences between an irreversible change and a reversible one.' I can't believe it. We've done all this in class, but I can't quite remember what's what.

Leader   Having trouble answering a question? Need a gentle reminder?

Pupil   What? Who? Yes, I do, actually, but where are you?

Leader   Not where but who – I'm a voice inside your head and my job is to sort out all the remembered bits of information. In every lesson, you take in certain facts and these are stored. Well, at the moment you've been taking in an awful lot of information in science and I'm here to help you figure out which bits you'll need to answer these questions.

Pupil   Great, then you answer this for me.

Leader   Wait just a second – I didn't say I'd do the questions for you. I said I'd help you remember what you know already. When you read the question to yourself, I try to pick out the important words and link them to what you've been doing in class. Let's have a look …

Show the question on the OHP/whiteboard.

Leader   OK, the important words here seem to be … I think I might need the science team for this one. (*Dials the science team.*)

Science team lazing around chatting.

ST 1   So anyway, I said to the boss, 'I'm fed up – there's too much thinking going on around here at the moment.'

ST 2   Yeah – we haven't been this busy since …

ST 3   Exactly – this has got to stop.

ST 4	We were promised a week's holiday this July, but now he's suggesting that even that might involve some work – I blame the teachers.
ST 5	Let's strike!
All	Yeah!
ST 5	You tell him!
ST 4	No, you tell him!
Leader	Tell me what, Number 4?
ST 4	Er, well do you expect us to work this hard all the time?
Leader	No, Number 4, I expect you to … ur … try a little harder, just until May, then you can switch off! Now, I have an important job for you. (………………) is having problems with this question – take a look.
ST 4	OK, OK, I think I understand. (…………………) has covered this in class not so long ago, and just needs our help to jog their memory. Well, where is (………………)?
Leader	Over there, now don't scare (him/her) – none of that.

Science Team come in chanting (cheerleader style)

Science Team	We're here to help you, we're your support! We're here to help you, we're your support! We're gonna help you remember what you've been taught! We're gonna help you remember what you've been taught!
Leader	Silence, science team. That was quite hard to say!
Pupil	More of you! Why are you here?
Science Team	We're here to help you, we're your support! We're here to help you, we're … .
Pupil	OK, OK, well get on with it then!

ST 1 That's gratitude for you! This question is about changes that happen to materials, in this case, the candle. There are two types of change. Let's take one at a time – first irreversible changes! We need some help here from the irreversible team. (*Whistles.*)

Five children come in, all dressed in the same colour (IRTs).

IRT 1 Hi! I'm part of the irreversible team. I'm going to need an egg, some bread and some sausages for this.

Pupil Wow – are you going to do an investigation?

IRT 1 No, I haven't had any breakfast yet this morning, and if we're going to get your memory going we're going to need some energy!

IRT 2 Right, eggs, bread, sausages. But how does this help us?

IRT 3 I think I know where this is going.

IRT 2 So do I! (*Starts to put fork in mouth.*)

IRT 1 (*Takes the plate of food away.*) At the moment, this food is uncooked – raw, in other words. You can't eat it like that.

IRT 4 But you can like this. (*Shows a plate of cooked food – this could be pretend food.*) What do you notice?

Pupil Well, it certainly looks different and it's hot.

IRT 5 That's right, it IS different. When it was heated, a chemical reaction took place and changed the material for good!

ST 1 So to recap, an irreversible change means that a chemical reaction has occurred and we can't get back the materials we first started with. (*Holds up 'Irreversible change' sign*)

Pupil Right, that's it. I remember now, thanks! Well, that means then that some changes CAN be reversed. It's all coming back to me.

Leader Don't be so sure! Let the reversible team remind you.

The reversible team (4 children) come walking in backwards with their clothes on back to front.

RT 1   Elbisrever era segnahc emos!

RT 2   I think what he's trying to say is that, some changes are reversible, just like that sentence!

RT 3   These changes can be easily reversed. In other words, you can get back the materials you started with.

RT 4   Can you think of any?

Pupil   Mmm … I know – like ice can change to water and back to ice again!

RT 4   That's right! What's that process called, when you start with a solid, like ice or chocolate, and it turns into a liquid? (*Asks the audience – 'melting'.*)

RT 4   Brilliant! But what needs to happen to the solid material for it to melt?

Pupil   I know – HEAT, it needs heat!

ST 2   Now we're getting somewhere! Particles – where are you?

6 children come in dressed in red, standing very close to each other.

ST 2   Make sure you don't mess this up – the boss is listening …

ST 1   PARTICLES, look at the state of you! (*Particles turn round to reveal the word solid.*)

Particles   We are in a solid state, sir!

ST 1   Well, pull yourselves together, then! Particles in solids are tightly packed! (*Children move closer together and link arms.*)

ST 2   So you see, in a solid, like ice, there's not much movement going on; but the minute you heat it up, watch what happens …

Particles get excited and jump about, but still holding hands.

ST 3   Now they can flow easily and fill any container (*addressing the audience*), so they must be a … (*'liquid'*).

2 narrators step forward.

Narrator 3   When a solid turns into a liquid, the process is called melting.

Narrator 4   If you make it colder again (let's say you were to put some water in the freezer), then the particles begin to slow down and move together again – this is freezing and you've got what you had to start with.

ST 3   Let's take it a stage further. Particles, show us what happens if we heat the liquid up.

Particles   We are in a liquid state. (*Pupils move around each other.*)

ST 4   Now, if we heat it up even further (boiling), these particles get even more excited and move apart even further.

Particles   We are in a gas state – we can move into any space. (*Pupils move around and apart.*)

Pupil   I know about this! This is called evaporation, but if you cool the gas particles down again so they reform into a liquid, that's condensation!

Leader   I can see you're remembering now, so let's recap everything:

Two more narrators step forward.

Narrator 5   We can have irreversible changes when we heat or burn materials such as food, meaning we cannot get back what we started with.

Narrator 6   And then there are reversible changes (like melting, freezing, evaporation and condensation), when the state is changed, but here we can get back what we started with.

Leader   There are other types of reversible changes, but we haven't got time for that.

Pupil   You've been a great help – I think I can answer the question now!

ST1   Excellent! Thank you for watching our assembly – we hope you enjoyed it!

Let's Investigate!

Subject: Science

Area of Study: Investigations (focusing on insulation)

Summary: Let Holmes and Watson guide you through a science investigation from the planning stage to the conclusion, with the help of a mad scientist, some pupils and a fortune-teller!

Timing: 10–15 minutes approx

Props:
- cups made of polystyrene, plastic and metal
- ball ● table and five chairs
- OHP/whiteboard ● words for sashes; 'Question', 'Planning', 'Prediction', 'Practical', 'Results' and 'Conclusion'

Music: None needed

Background Work:
- Knowledge of the investigative process, focusing on insulation

Cast and costumes:

Part	No needed	Suggested costumes
Narrators	2	School uniform/clothing
Holmes	1	Tweed jacket, trousers, white shirt, pipe, magnifying glass, hat
Watson	1	See Holmes
Pupils presenting planning stage	5	School uniform/clothing
Pupils presenting results and conclusion	5	School uniform/clothing
Mad Scientist	1	Stereotypical scientists' uniform – white coat etc
Assistant	1	Stereotypical scientists' uniform – white coat etc
Fortune-teller	1	Flowing material with sun, moon and star patterns to suggest an air of mystery
Pupils with sashes	6	School uniform/clothing, material for sashes

Suggested Script – Let's Investigate

Narrator 1   Welcome to our assembly. We would like to tell you a bit about science investigations.

Sherlock Holmes and Watson walk on, Watson with a big magnifying glass and Holmes with a pipe.

Watson   So Holmes, why do we bother investigating, spending hour after hour puzzling, predicting and proving?

Holmes   Elementary, my dear Watson! It isn't only us who investigate. Lots of people, every day, solve some kind of problem. Watch this.

Narrator 2   Here's what we think an investigation is all about ...

Mad Scientist   Good morning to you all. I am Professor You Can't Tell Me Anything I Don't Know Already. First of all, there has to be a problem to solve. Some kind of question to answer ...

Pupil 1   I know, Professor You Can't Tell Me Anything I Don't Know Already! How is it that teachers always have to be right and why do we have to have homework?

Assistant whispers to Mad Scientist.

Mad Scientist   Well, I am not at liberty to answer those questions. Moving swiftly on! Seriously, though, you have to have a question to get the ball rolling.

A ball rolls across the stage. 2 children holding up a banner with the word 'Question' on it walk across the stage followed by a group of children gestering a pondering pose.

Pupil 2   In class, we were given this problem to solve: 'A fast-food restaurant has had complaints from its customers saying that their tea was getting cold too quickly. Devise an investigation that can give an answer as to which material will keep the tea hottest.'

Pupil 3   Right, then, let's get the equipment out and start testing!

Mad Scientist   STOP, STOP! Before you can do any of that, you have to have some kind of plan! Goodness me! What am I working with? Amateurs! Over to my assistant, Doctor Who Knows Slightly Less Than I Do!

A banner with the word 'Planning' is displayed across the stage.

Assistant   Right, well then. These are just some questions you will need to answer to bring your plan into action …

Reads out the problem about the tea getting cold in a very boring way. (The whole question could be displayed on an OHP/whiteboard for all pupils to read.)

'A fast-food restaurant has had complaints from its customers saying that their tea was getting cold too quickly. Devise an investigation that can give an answer as to which material will keep the tea hottest.

So, for our experiment, there are several things we need to look at before we begin. What sort of things do we need to keep the same?

Pupil 4   The size of the cups, the amount of water, the starting temperature of the water. We could use boiling water from the kettle as long as we are careful.

Assistant   Very good – and what do we need to change?

Pupil 4   This boring person reading out the questions!

Assistant   Before I was so rudely interrupted! What do we need to change?

Pupil 5   The material of the cups, of course. We need to find out which material is the best insulator (plastic, polystyrene or metal).

Pupil 3   As well as this, we will need a list of the equipment we're going to use and a basic outline of what you're going to do.

Mad Scientist   The next stage …

Fortune-teller   (*Using a French accent.*) I see a child wearing red (*or whatever colour the school uniform is*).

Mad Scientist   Oh no! Whose idea was this? I see 200 children wearing red, what of it?

Fortune-teller   Do not break my concentration!

Assistant   That wouldn't take an awful lot, would it!

Fortune-teller   I see a child wearing (…………). And the number five. There is a house with a blue door … .

Mad Scientist	This is going a little too far, don't you think? After all, we are only predicting what will happen in the investigation. Thank you, Fortune-teller! Your services are no longer required.

Banner with the word 'Prediction' is displayed across the stage.

Pupil 2	We have to predict which material (polystyrene, plastic or metal) will keep the water the hottest. Can we now carry out the practical side of the investigation?

Mad Scientist	Yes, yes, but safely and accurately.

Banner with the word 'Practical' is carried across the stage by 2 children.

Pupil 6	We have already done this investigation and came up with these results.

Banner with word 'Results' is displayed across the stage. (Show the results of your experiment using OHP'/whiteboard.)

Pupil 7	From the results we were able to draw a graph. Here it is. (*Display graph on OHP/whiteboard.*)

Watson	Phew, that took an awfully long time to get through, but at least they have an answer now.

Holmes	Not quite, Watson! They need to understand the graph so that they can answer their question.

Mad Scientist	Now, we need to understand the graph so that we can answer the question, which was ...

Pupil 8	Which material will keep the tea the hottest?

Banner with word 'Conclusion' is displayed across the stage.

Pupil 9	We concluded from our investigation that polystyrene kept the tea the hottest, so this is the material that the fast-food restaurant should use. (*Show why using graph on OHP/whiteboard.*)

Watson	Fantastic, very interesting.

Holmes	Yes, Watson ... you have so much more to learn!

Watson	Do you fancy a cup of tea at the local tea-room, Holmes?

Holmes	Not that one, no. I hear they use metal cups!

Pupil 10	That's it! Thanks for listening. We hope you enjoyed it.

Water, Water, Everywhere!

Subject: Science

Area of Study: The water cycle

Summary: An opportunity to see exactly what happens in the water cycle from the point of view of two water droplets, Drip and Drop! Join with them as they explain why water is so important and where it comes from.

Timing: 20 minutes approx

Props:
- bicycle
- large diagram/picture of the water cycle
- bottle of water
- magnifying glass
- CD player
- drum
- cymbal
- signs; 'Drip'. 'Drop'

Music: *Here Comes the Sun* by Nina Simone

Background Work:
- Work on the water cycle

Cast and costumes:

Part	No needed	Suggested costumes
Narrators	7	School uniform/clothing
Drip	1	Blue shorts/trousers and a blue top. Blue hat, and sign with 'Drip' pinned to top
Drop	1	As above, but with 'Drop' pinned to top
Scientists	4	Stereotypical scientists' uniform – white coat etc
Particles	5	PE kit
Audience members	3	School uniform/clothing (these children are sitting in the audience)
Comedians	3	School uniform/clothing, bow tie and optional wig
Cyclist	1	PE kit or, if available, cyclist gear and equipment
The Sun	1	Yellow clothes – perhaps yellow face paint or hat

Suggested Script – Water, Water Everywhere

Narrator 1 Welcome to our assembly (*voice becomes quieter and quieter as he speaks*). We have been revising solids, liquids and gases in science and decided to … (*drops head and 'switches off'*).

Narrator 2 (*Grins at audience and looks worriedly at person next to them.*) Erm, I'm sorry about this, it looks as if … he has switched off. (*Looks to the left and right.*)

(*Drip and Drop enter stage, peering at them both.*)

Drip Drip. Oh. Look how worried he looks. Do you think there's something wrong?

Drop Drop. What do you think – he/she looks worried about something.

Drip Drip. No need for that …

Drop Drop. Don't be so wet, then. Let's ask.

Drip Drip. What's wrong?

Narrator 2 It's a bit embarrassing, really. We're trying to do our assembly, our parents are here and everything and (………………) decided to switch off. I don't know what's wrong with him/her.

Drip Drip. Mmmm … Showing classic signs of dehydration.

Narrator 2 Dehy…hy what? And why do you keep saying 'drip'?

Drop Drop. De-hy-dra-tion. It means that your friend probably hasn't had enough water this morning to keep him/her going.

Narrator 2 Why is water so important? And why do YOU keep saying 'drop'?

Drop Drop. So many questions, so little time. Let's start with the easy ones. My name's Drop and his name is Drip. We're water droplets in the air.

Narrator 2 So why can I see you, then?

Drip Drip. Normally you can't; we're tiny. But we saw what your class has been doing and thought we'd help out.

Drop Drop. Did you know that there's usually about 3 100 cubic miles of us in the air at any one time?

Narrator 2 No, that's fascinating, (*voice fading*) but I really need to carry on with … (*Switches off too.*)

Brilliant Publications © Katie Harris and Amanda MacNaughton

Drip	Drip. There goes another one. When will they learn? Humans need water to keep them alive and healthy. I think we had better take it from here. Let's sit them down with some water.
Drop	Drop. Water is colourless.
Drip	Drip. Water is odourless.
Drop	Drop. Water is tasteless. Remind me again why they decided to look at water. It doesn't sound particularly interesting.
Scientist 1	Do you mind? Water is vital to life, AQUA VITA! Did you know that 75% of the Earth's surface is water?
Scientist 2	And there is much more water under our feet!
Scientist 3	More importantly, we need to drink plenty of water every day too, because our body is 60% water and it constantly needs topping up!
Scientist 4	Time for one last fact! 70% of your brain is water. That's why you need a drink to help you think.
Drip	Drip. Thank you for that. H_2O is very important for lots …
Drop	Drop. H_2 …
Drip	Drip. Bless you. Now if you don't mind …
Drop	Drop. I meant, what is H_2O? It sounds like YOU need some water. We're supposed to be talking about water, not H_2O.
Drip	Drip. You must have water in your ears! H_2O IS WATER, you drip!
Drop	Drop. No, I'm Drop.
Drip	Drip. Very funny. H_2O is the special scientific symbol for water. Now, I think it's time we opened up.
Drop	Drop. Pardon? If you have problems, now's not the time.
Drip	Drip. I mean, I think it's time we let these people take a closer look at us. (*Holds magnifying glass up at Drop.*)
Drop	Drop. I'm not liking this, but I think our jokes are drying up, so I'll go with it.

Drip holds up giant magnifying glass in front of Drop. Drop stands to one side and in his place are particles.

All Particles   We are particles of water!

Particle 1   I am a particle.

Particle 2   I am another particle.

Particle 3   I am also a particle.

Particle 4   Yes, you guessed it, I am a particle too.

Particle 5   No, you're not, you're Particle 4. Anyway, I am a more important particle because I have more to say.

All Particles   We are in a liquid state.

Particle 5   We can fill any container you pour us into.

Particle 4   If you heat us up, even a little bit, we get quite excited.

All Particles   Yeah. Heat us up! Heat us up!

Particle 5   We begin to move around more and space out.
(*Particles move around and away from each other.*)

All Particles   When we are heated.

Narrator 3   They turn from a LIQUID into a GAS. This process is called EVAPORATION.

Particle 3   We rise up into the air, cos that's what we do when we get too hot, then as we begin to cool down …

Particles move together and hold hands.

All Particles   We become a liquid again.

Narrator 4   When a GAS cools down and becomes a LIQUID, the process is called CONDENSATION.

Narrator 5   You can often see this happening.

Narrator 6   If you breathe out on a cold day, you will see your breath – this is the warm air from your mouth turning into liquid water in the air, called water vapour.

Narrator 7   Or, if you boil a kettle near a window. You can see the hot steam hit the cold window, and condensation has happened. The gas or steam has turned into a liquid – water droplets on the window.

Particle 5   Yes, thank you, this is our bit! Now we are a liquid and you cool us down even more – like put us in a freezer. Then we slow down even more, moving closer together.

Particles move closer together and link arms.

All Particles   Now we are a solid – ICE. We have frozen.

Narrator 1   What? Who? Where? Who are you?

Drip   Drip. Don't worry about that now; have another drink of water.

Narrator 1   But I'm supposed to be telling everyone where water comes from.

Drip   Drip. It's all under control – you could say we have a water-tight plan!

Drop   Drop. Groan, groan. There are some children who look quite alert – let's ask them to do the next bit. You, you and you – can you make your way up here, please?

3 children come up from the audience.

Audience 1   I really don't think …

Drip   Drip. Of course you can. Have a look at this for a few minutes while we keep everyone entertained. (*Hands children from audience a sheet with their script on.*)

3 comedians come on stage.

Comedian 1   Doctor, doctor, I think I've been bitten by a vampire. Here, have a drink of water. Will this make me better? No, but I'll be able to see if your neck leaks.

2 hits of a drum, then a cymbal.

Comedian 2   A man was crawling across the desert as thirsty as he could be when he saw a man in the distance. As the man approached, he said, 'Would you like to buy a tie?' 'No' said the man, 'But do you have any water? I'm really thirsty.' 'No water, but I do have a lovely selection of ties.' He walked off and the unfortunate man was left crawling in the sun until he came to a hotel. He crawled up the steps, crying, 'Water! Water!' The manager approached him and said, 'I'm sorry, Sir, but you can't come in here without a tie!'

2 hits of a drum, then a cymbal.

Comedian 3   A son says to his Dad, 'Dad, Dad, there's a woman collecting for the town's new swimming pool.' So the dad replied, 'Well, give her a glass of water, then!'

© Katie Harris and Amanda MacNaughton   **Brilliant Publications**

Drip	Drip. Enough, enough! When you're ready … and action!
Audience 1	We've heard about why we need water and how it can change. But where exactly do we get it from?
Audience 2	Well, that's easy. Rivers, seas, oceans, lakes.
Drip	Drip. No improvising, please; just read what's there.
Audience 2	Sorry. But why are you telling them something they already know?
Drop	Drop. OK, Mr/Miss Clever Clogs, why haven't the rivers and oceans all dried up then?
Audience 2	Because as it rains and snows, it keeps them topped up.
Drip	Drip. So the water doesn't come from the rivers and lakes then, like you said before?
Audience 2	Well, yes it does but …
Audience 3	Stop! We just seem to be going round in circles.
Drip	Drip. Exactly.
Audience 3	What do you mean?
Audience 1	He means that it is a continuous cycle.

Someone rides in on a bike.

Audience 1	The water cycle. You're going to need those particles back again to explain this one!
Scientist 1	Let's start here because this is where there is most water. Particles, you are in a liquid state.

Particles stand in a liquid state (holding hands).

Scientist 2	Imagine you are a particle near the surface of a lake, ocean or river. There you are, minding your own business, when the sun comes out …

Music is switched on, Here Comes The Sun.

Sun	Let me shed some light on this. I gently warm the Earth and water, and, as I do, those particles near the surface begin to …

All Particles	GET EXCITED AND MOVE AROUND! (*Move around area as far apart as possible.*)
Sun	Yes, that's right. And we know what happens next …
All Particles	WE MOVE APART AND BECOME A GAS!
Scientist 3	(*Pointing to water cycle diagram.*) They move apart and become a gas. Those tiny particles rise up from the water and into the atmosphere. Can anyone remember what the process is called? (*Asks the audience.*) That's right, EVAPORATION.
Scientist 4	Clouds are formed as they rise up and then they start to cool down.
Sun	And we know what that means …
All Particles	We slow down and move closer together. (*Begin by touching fingertips and move to holding hands.*)
Scientist 4	They move closer together to become a liquid. Can anyone remember what this process is? (*Asks the audience again.*) Ah, good, CONDENSATION.
Drip	Drip. OK – we'll take it from here. (*Everyone sits down.*)
Drop	Drop. Drip. Did you have to be so rude?
Drip	Drip. Drop.
Drop	Drop. Drip.
Drip	Drip. Now look what you've started.
Drop	Drop. When the water becomes too heavy it falls as rain, and if it becomes even colder it falls as snow.
Narrator 1	What on earth is going on?
Narrator 2	I don't know, but we'd better get this assembly started.
Narrator 1	Welcome to our assembly.
Drip	Drip. It's all finished. We've done it for you.
Drop	Drop. And we've got to be somewhere else. It's getting very warm in here, and we need to be off to higher places.
Drip	Drip. (*Turns to audience.*) Thanks for listening.

Rapid River Research!

Subject:	Geography
Area of Study:	Rivers

Summary:

A class of children are studying rivers and are taken on a field trip to carry out some practical work. This is a 'fast-flowing' assembly packed full of facts and suggestions about how not to get into 'deep water' on such a trip!

Timing: 20–25 minutes approx

Props:

- Pictures of the water cycle   • bamboo stick
- metre stick   • trundle wheel
- long reel of blue paper (backing) or material   • stopwatch
- clipboards   • clear plastic bottles   • marker pen
- signs: 'The following week', 'Meander', 'Tributary', 'Floodplain', 'Waterfall', 'Source', 'Mouth' (and others, if required)

Music: *Water of Life* and other music linked to rivers

Background Work:

- Science – the water cycle
- Art – sketches/paintings of a river showing perspective or showing the different features of the surrounding countryside
- Geography – features of a river, some knowledge of safety by a riverside and river pollution, ideas for how to save water

Cast and costumes:

Part	No needed	Suggested costumes
Narrator	1	School uniform/clothing
Teacher/TA	2	Shirt, smart trousers/skirt, glasses on a chain, wellies and coat for field trip
Pupils	Any number	School uniform/clothing, wellies and coats for field trip

Brilliant Publications

Suggested Script–Rapid River Research!

Narrator 1   Welcome to our assembly. We have been learning all about rivers and would like to share some of our learning with you.

Mrs Ippi is at the front of the class talking to her pupils about their topic of rivers and showing them some pictures of the water cycle.

Mrs Ippi   So class, where does the water actually come from?

Pupil 1   From the sky, Miss?

Pupil 2   From clouds, Miss, when it rains?

Pupil 3   I thought it came from the ground, Miss, you know from natural springs underground.

Pupil 4   We get our water from the tap!

Mrs Ippi   Well, the good thing is, children, none of you are wrong. As this picture shows (*holds up poster of the water cycle*), water travels and changes all the time – it's an amazing thing.

Mrs Ippi calls up a few children, one at a time, to explain what is happening in each part of the water cycle.

Pupil 5   Well, here the water is being evaporated by the sun, and the water vapour (tiny water droplets – invisible to the eye) is travelling upwards.

Pupil 6   The clouds are formed when the water vapour becomes cold enough to condense. It turns back to a liquid, then, when the cloud is heavy enough, it rains.

Pupil 7   The rain falls to the ground, on trees, back into rivers and streams, all over the place, really. Some of it is absorbed by the ground where it falls and some of it flows back into the rivers.

Mrs Ippi   Fantastic! Now let's think about some of those rivers, shall we? What rivers do you know of?

Pupil 8   The Mississippi, Mrs Ippi? (*They all giggle.*)

Mrs Ippi   Well, I thought that might be one of the first suggestions! Any others? Yes, Dan?

Pupil 9   The Danube, Miss?
(Dan)

Mrs Ippi	Absolutely! Niall?
Pupil 10 (Niall)	Uh … Oh! Of course. The Nile, Miss!
Mrs Ippi	Yes! What about one a bit closer to home, then?
Pupil 11	The River (........................), Miss! (*Can use the name of a local river or make one up.*)
Mrs Ippi	Yes! And that, children, is where we are going on our field trip next week.

As child walks across stage holding sign saying 'The following week', pupils and teachers put on their wellies, macs and find their clipboards. Between them they carry a metre stick, a bamboo, a marker pen, a trundle wheel, a stopwatch, a couple of glass/clear plastic jars. The children walk along behind two teachers until they stop. At the back of the stage, 2 children are holding a long reel of blue paper/material stretched across its width to represent the river.

Mrs Ippi	Right, Miss Ouri is going to carefully go into the river – something only an adult should do – and measure how deep it is with this piece of bamboo.
Miss Ouri	Oooh, it's pretty cold – being a TA, I get all the best jobs!

Miss Ouri wades into the water (goes behind the blue material/paper), puts the bamboo into the water and, using a marker pen, measures where the water reaches. She passes the bamboo to one of the children.

Miss Ouri	Right, Dan, can you use the metre stick to measure how far that water came up, please? Then we'll know how deep this river is.

Dan does the measuring and reads the depth out to everyone, who then write it down on their clipboards.

Meanwhile, 3 children (Pupils 12, 13 & 14) start at one end of the river. 1 child remains there whilst the others use the trundle wheel to measure out 5 or 10 metres. When they stop, the child at the start drops a big stick into the river and shouts 'GO!' One of the other 2 starts the stopwatch. When the stick reaches the end of the 5/10 metres (it could be pulled by a thin piece of thread!), a child shouts 'STOP!' and the stopwatch is stopped.

Pupil 12   OK, now we can calculate the speed of the river! Um … I'm not sure how to do the maths though! (*Looks to Pupil 13.*)

Pupil 13   Well, don't look at me – I'm no number cruncher … (*Looks to Pupil 14.*)

Pupil 14   Well, it's something to do with the distance and the time it takes to … oh, I don't know.

Pupils 12, 13 & 14   (*Shouting.*) MAXIMILLIAN!

Pupil 15 Max   (*Comes running over, busily scribbling on his clipboard.*) Yes?

Pupil 13   We need your expert number skills, Max – can you calculate the speed of this river with these timings and distances?

Max   Oh … yes, yes, of course, just a minute … (*mutters numbers and long words like 'velocity' to himself.*) This river is travelling at 0.6 metres per second!

Everybody writes this down on their clipboard, except for 2 children who have sneaked away from the group on their own.

Pupil 16   Boring! Boring! Boring! I thought we might be doing something exciting, like seeing who could get from one side to the other the quickest or standing in the river and seeing who could catch the biggest frog!

Pupil 17   Ugh! Well, I'm glad we're not doing that, but it is SO dull here; there's nothing to do … . I'm thirsty too – have you got any drink left? I had all of mine on the coach!

Pupil 16   No, me too … could we just get some from the river?

Pupil 17   I'm not drinking it if it looks dirty – put some in this bottle and let's have a look at it.

They collect some water in a clear plastic bottle and hold it up to the light – they both peer it at carefully.

Pupil 16   Looks perfectly clear to me – nothing in it but water!

Pupil 17   Hmmm ... I can't see anything either – must be OK to drink then! (*Begins to take a drink when suddenly another child comes running over.*)

Pupil 18   Oy! You two! Quick! Mrs Ippi's going out of her mind 'cos you two have disappeared.

They go running back to the group to find Mrs Ippi and Miss Ouri looking furious.

Mrs Ippi   What have I told you before about staying with the group (..................)? I just hope you haven't been up to any mischief! Now, we were just about to collect some water from the river to take back to the class for testing, so you can both help. (*Takes the water bottle from Pupils 16 and 17.*)

Pupil 16   Testing? What do you mean ... testing?

Miss Ouri   For goodness' sake, boys, do you ever listen? We all know that river water can be polluted – that's why you should never drink any straight out of the river. As part of our science topic, we're going to carry out some tests when we get back to the classroom to see exactly what kind of pollution is in our local river! But before we go, let's do some sketching.

Pupils 16 and 17 look at each other in shock; Pupil 17 puts his hand to his stomach with a worried look! Everyone settles down on the ground with their clipboards and begins to sketch the river and the countryside as the two teachers wander around looking at their work.

Mrs Ippi   Lovely! Lovely! Just think what a beautiful display this will make, Miss Ouri!

Miss Ouri   I know – I can just picture it!

A piece of music is played (can be something linked to Rivers, something classical), whilst children move slowly around the two teachers holding their river pictures/ paintings out in front of them for the audience to see. Children could be directed by Miss Ouri to stand in a certain place (as if creating the classroom display).

When the music finishes, the children go back to their sitting positions for sketching, and both teachers begin to ask them questions about the features of a river.

NOTE: This section of the assembly can be lengthened or shortened to include more or fewer features according to the time available.

Mrs Ippi Do you know what this part here is, where it bends round?

2 children stand at the front, one who holds up the sign naming the feature and the other who reads out the definition of the feature.

Pupil 1	MEANDER
Pupil 2	Bends in the river to avoid obstacles like trees.
Miss Ouri	Where does this river actually start – can you see?
Pupil 1	SOURCE
Pupil 2	Where a river starts – it may be from rain falling on a hilltop or water welling up from underground.
Mrs Ippi	Oh, well done (...................); you've shown a tributary on yours.
Pupil 1	TRIBUTARY
Pupil 2	A stream that flows into the river – some are small and others are rivers in their own right!
Miss Ouri	Now this river hasn't got any waterfalls that we can see, but many do.
Pupil 1	WATERFALL
Pupil 2	Where a river plummets over a step of hard rock.
Maximillian	Look, Miss, I've remembered to include a floodplain in my drawing!
Pupil 1	FLOODPLAIN
Pupil 2	Rivers can carry loads of mud, soil and sand as they move. A floodplain is where the river decides to dump all that mud and stuff before carrying on with its journey.
Mrs Ippi	And can anybody tell me what it's called when the river joins the sea?
Pupil 1	MOUTH
Pupil 2	Where the river flows into a sea – the journey's end!
Mrs Ippi	And the end of our trip, I'm afraid, children – time to go!

The children collect their things and go back to their classroom places while a child walks across the stage with a sign saying 'The following week'.

As the children move back to their classroom places, 'Water of Life' begins to play – all children including teacher sing either all or part of the song.

Mrs Ippi	Well, it's good to see you back, (...*Pupil 17*...). What's been the matter?
Pupil 17	Stomach bug, Miss!

Mrs Ippi   You missed a lot of the work following our field trip, including the results of our pollution tests on the river water, which is a shame. Can anybody tell (...Pupil 17...) the types of things we found were polluting our water?

Various pupils Sewage! ... dead animals! ... fertilizers! ... even dog wee!

Pupil 17 looks more horrified with each answer.

Pupil 17   Uh, Miss, actually I still don't feel that great – I think I might be sick again (*runs off stage*).

Mrs Ippi   Oh dear! Now, in that song we were just singing, think about the line 'There's a busy workman digging in the desert, digging in the sand where nothing much grows.' Now, as many of you know from your river projects, there are places in the world that suffer from drought, where the rivers dry up and nothing grows and there are also places where there is flooding, and houses and lives are ruined. Today I want us all to think of a way in which we can save on the amount of water we use.

Each child in turn stands up and completes the sentence ...

'To save water I am going to ... .'
(*Have showers instead of baths, or turn the tap off when I'm brushing my teeth.*)

Miss Ouri   Wow, children, you've really inspired me – well done!

Narrator 1   We hope we have inspired you too – thank you for watching our assembly!

Wish You Were Here ... in St Lucia

Subject: Geography

Area of Study: St Lucia

Summary: A life-size banana, a pawpaw and a hotel manager help Johnny, who is always falling asleep in class, discover and appreciate the beautiful island of St Lucia.

Timing: 15–20 minutes approx

Props:
- OHP/whiteboard ● costumes (see below)
- bananas ● rubber ring ● cocktail-type glass

Music: None needed

Background Work:
- Map work on St Lucia
- Comparative graphs showing temperature and rainfall of St Lucia and the UK
- Adverts/postcards highlighting appealing features of the island

Cast and costumes:

Part	No needed	Suggested costumes
Pilot	1	No uniform needed, as voice part only – child stands to the side and is voice of the pilot
Johnny	1	School uniform/clothing
Pupils 2, 3, 4, 5, 6	5	School uniform/clothing
Teacher	1	Smart clothes (eg trousers, shirt and tie, or skirt and blouse)
Banana (Bruce)	1	This could be as elaborate or as simple as you want it to be, eg yellow hat and clothes with cut-out banana shapes stuck all over clothes
Pawpaw	1	Orangey T-shirt, shorts/leggings, accessories!
Facts 1, 2, 3	3	School uniform/clothing
Baby bananas	3	As banana costume
Pete Ton	1	Smart clothes

Suggested Script – Wish You Were Here ... in St Lucia

Chairs arranged in twos to resemble the seating on an aeroplane. Sitting on the chairs 4 children in school uniform and their teacher wearing a sunhat and glasses, holding a rubber ring and a cocktail glass.

Pilot   Flight 21478 for St Lucia will shortly be arriving at Hewanorra International Airport. Please fasten your seatbelts and prepare for landing.

Johnny   I still can't believe that (*...name of the headteacher...*) has actually agreed to pay for the whole of our year group to come to St Lucia as part of our geography.

Pupil 2   Just think of all those watersports we can do – it's going to be great!

Pupil 3   I do think that (*...name of class teacher...*) has taken it a little bit too far. Anyone would think that teachers don't have time for holidays!

Johnny   No school for two whole weeks!

Johnny puts his hands behind his head and closes his eyes.

Pupil dressed as teacher with rubber ring quickly gets up, takes off accessories and appears at the front of what is now the class.

Teacher   Are we keeping you up, Johnny? Wake up!

Johnny   What? Eh? Are we there yet?

Teacher   No, break-time is a long way off, and even further for you now! Now, as I was saying ... Well, maybe (.................) can recap for me.

Pupil 4   St Lucia is an island that can be found in the Caribbean Sea. Here it is.

OHP/whiteboard or large map showing a simple map of St Lucia.

Pupil 5   It is a volcanic island, which means that millions of years ago, volcanoes erupted under the sea again and again to form the island. These mountains are called the Pitons.

Pupil 4   Because of the fertile soil, St Lucia is rich in beautiful tropical plants and animals. One of the most important of these is the banana plant.

Johnny dozes off again and a life-size banana taps him on the back. He gets up and walks into the middle.

Banana   Hey there, Johnny! The name's Anana Banana, but you can call me Bruce. Before you ask, no, I'm not real, you're daydreaming again. So I thought I might help you get through this and have some fun along the way.

Johnny   (*Slowly*) OK. (*Can't quite believe what is happening.*)

Banana   I know how much you hate hard work, so I've asked some friends to help me, while you sit back and enjoy!

Child dressed as pawpaw walks into the hall as if he/she has some kind of celebrity status. Children clap and whistle, excited to see him/her.

Pawpaw   (*Dramatically*) Yes, I'm here, the star of the show ... just in case you've not heard of me, I'm Pawpaw, so cool they named me twice!

Johnny   Now I've seen everything!

Banana   Give him a chance; he's more than just a badly named fruit, you know!

Pawpaw   Why aren't bananas ever lonely? Because they come in bunches!

Banana   Er, sorry to rush you, but can we ...

Pawpaw   Fine, it's you who's missing out. There are lots of differences between the UK and St Lucia. Can you think of any?

Johnny   Well, St Lucia is hot and the UK, well, isn't?

Pawpaw   (*Sarcastically*) You're sharp, that's for sure! The UK has a climate of warm summers, when we're lucky, and cool winters, whereas St Lucia is hot all year round. Have a look at these graphs that your classmates have put together.

2 pupils come out and display a graph (could be Powerpoint/OHP/whiteboard/large-scale drawing) showing average temperature over a year for the UK and St Lucia. Briefly state the differences.

Johnny   I remember doing these; I think we looked at rainfall as well. That's right, St Lucia is really dry and the UK is really wet.

Pawpaw   Bruce, does he sleep through EVERY lesson? Anyway, listen carefully to what these children have to say.

2 pupils come out and display a graph (could be Powerpoint/OHP/whiteboard/large-scale drawing) showing average rainfall over a year for the UK and St Lucia. Briefly state the differences.

Pawpaw   I'm going to have to go – everyone's getting together at a place called 'The Smoothie' later on. Sounds good. Are you coming, Bruce?

Banana   I might give it a miss. I'm not one for extreme sports, but thanks for the invitation!
(*Pauses*)
I think it's time for fast and furious postcard facts!

For each fact, child runs to middle of performing area and reads out fact, then rushes off the other side.

Fact 1   Did you know that most of the roads and villages on St Lucia are situated along the coast because of the mountainous terrain?

Fact 2   The capital city of St Lucia is Castries and approximately 50 000 people live there.

Fact 3   Two of the major industries in St Lucia are the fruit and vegetable industry, in particular bananas, and the tourist industry.

Banana   We're going to have a look at these two industries, starting with my favourite, growing and selling bananas. (*Looking at the side of the room.*) In you come, don't be shy.

3 baby bananas shuffle into the middle of the performing area, looking down at the floor.

Banana   Remember to speak up!

Baby Banana 1   Bananas grow in bunches on trees. First, they cut the bananas down and dry them.

Baby Banana 2   Next, they wash the bananas and pack them ready to be taken to the docks.

Baby Banana 3   Finally, we're loaded onto ships, taken all around the world and sold.

Johnny   I do love a nice banana split with chocolate sauce or a banana smoothie or even a …

Baby bananas run off crying.

Banana	That's enough of that kind of language, if you don't mind! I think I need to sit down for a while. I 'll let Pete explain the rest! A smoothie of all things, it's just like being in a horror movie! (*Sits down, shaking his head.*)

Pete Ton, hotel manager, dressed smartly, walks slowly forward.

Pete Ton	So you're Johnny, are you?
Johnny	Yes; who are you?
Pete Ton	(*speaks in a flat, unexciting voice*) I'm Pete, Pete Ton.
Johnny	Don't tell me, you're a giant parrot or another life-size fruit!
Pete Ton	No, I'm one of the hotel managers on the island. I'm here to tell you about the other major industry that provides a lot of jobs on St Lucia – tourism. People love coming to our island; in fact, more and more come each year. Just take a look at some of the reasons why.

3 or 4 children come up and show or read articles/adverts/postcards that they have completed in class about St Lucia, highlighting why it is such a tourist trap. While this is happening, Johnny sits back in his seat.

Pete Ton	So you see, it's a great place to visit. Mind you, too many tourists isn't always a good thing. Can you think why?
Johnny	Well, the noise pollution from hotels, boats and bars. Oh, and plants and animals are destroyed to build all the hotels, and then I suppose there's all the rubbish produced.
Banana	Looks like this sleep is doing you good! Thanks, Pete. I think it's time for me to split as it looks like your teacher is about to ...
Teacher	Not again! Wakey, wakey, Johnny! Where have you been?
Johnny	Well, there's a story!
Teacher	It'll have to wait 'til lunch time, when you come back for detention!
Pupil 6	Thanks for watching our assembly!

Climb Every Mountain

Subject: Geography

Area of Study: Mountains

Summary: Learn about the highs and lows of mountain life through this staged assembly, brought to you by wannabe presenters. This is an opportunity to present the facts and figures of mountains, from different perspectives.

Timing: 20 minutes approx

Props:
- map of the world
- labels: Mt Everest, Aconcagua, Denali, M
- hard-boiled egg
- diagrams of basic 'zones' of a mountain
- signs: 'Auditions this way' and 'Snow leopard'

Music: None needed

Background Work:
- Posters showing how mountains are formed
- Posters to warn people of the dangers of avalanches/landslides
- Knowledge of major world mountains and mountainous environments

Cast and costumes:

Part	No needed	Suggested costumes
Director	1	Smart clothes/school uniform
Casting Director	1	As above
Actors	5	School uniform
Clowns	2	Colourful clothes, red nose, novelty hair, clown accessories
Dr Rock	1	Hard hat, tools, dressed to look like a geologist out in the field
Ben Nevis	1	As above
Mountains	6	White top, green trousers, white cap
Snow leopard	1	Leopard mask, white clothes with spots
Mountain goats (could add more non-speaking goats)	4	Goat mask with horns, grey/brown clothes
Child to work OHP/whiteboard	1	School uniform

Suggested Script – Climb Every Mountain

Performing area set up as an auditioning room. Desk at the side for the Director and Casting Director; sign that says 'Auditions this way'.

Actor 1   (*In a very flat, boring voice*) Welcome. We would like to tell you all about mountains, where they are in the world, how they are formed and what a mountainous environment is.

Director   CUT! I've seen enough!

Casting Dir   NEXT!

Actor walks off and sits down.

Actor 2   (*Dressed in a nun's outfit and singing*) The hills are alive with the sound of ...

Director   STOP! You're in the wrong place! We're looking for presenters for our new documentary on mountains, not failed X-Factor contestants!

Casting Dir   NEXT!

Two clowns walk onto the middle of the performing area.

Clown 1   Why don't mountains get cold in the winter?

Clown 2   I don't know. Why don't mountains get cold in the winter?

Clown 1   Because they wear snow caps! (*Both laugh loudly at their own joke.*)

Director   That's it! Please go away! (*Clowns walk off. Turns to Casting Director*) I don't think we're ever going to find the presenters we're looking for at this rate.

Casting Dir   Wait a minute; they look hopeful. (*Two sensibly dressed actors walk forward*) OK, when you're ready, off you go.

Actor 3   We need to start with some basic facts. Did you know that 1/5 of the land's surface is mountains?

Actor 4   And a lot of our fresh water originates from mountains?

Actor 3   A mountain is generally over 330 m high. Anything less than that is classed as a hill.

© Katie Harris and Amanda MacNaughton

Director   At last! That was clear, concise and just what we're looking for. You're in. Please take a seat.

Casting Dir   Next we have a Dr Rock and his/her assistant, Ben Nevis.

Two geologists walk in.

Dr Rock   (*Smooth talker, very sure of him/herself*). Hi there! I'm Dr Rock. There's not much that I don't know about the Earth's surface – my knowledge is pretty rock-solid. (*Laughs to him/herself*). This is my assistant, Ben.

Ben Nevis   We're here to tell you how mountains are formed.

Dr Rock   Have you got that egg, Ben?

Ben passes Dr Rock the egg and, as he does, it drops on the ground. It's a hard-boiled egg, and so it's only the shell that's broken.

Dr Rock   (*Looks at audience*) Don't be shell-shocked; that's just how we need it. This egg is just like the Earth.

Ben Nevis   Well, the Earth is bigger than that, (...first name...).

Dr Rock   (*Sarcastically*) Do you think, Ben?! (*Gives a look to the audience*).

Ben Nevis   Well, it must be, because ...

Dr Rock   Anyway, the soft middle of the egg is like the Earth's middle or core, constantly moving around. The hard, broken shell on top is just like the plates that move around. They are also constantly moving and sometimes they collide or hit each other.

Ben Nevis   When this happens, mountains can be formed. But it takes millions of years.

(At this point, if the children have created posters to show how mountains are formed, they could be displayed on the walls around the hall.)

Director   Now we're talking – these guys really know their stuff.

Casting Dir   You've got it. Thank you; please sit down.

The two clowns from before walk on again.

Clown 1	Knock, knock.
Clown 2	Who's there?
Clown 1	Sheila.
Clown 2	Sheila who?
Clown 1	(*Singing*) Sheila be coming round the mountain when she comes, Sheila be ...
Director	Security! (*Clowns run off and sit down.*)
Casting Dir	Right! Next we have some mountains representing different ranges from around the world ... oh dear, shall we just skip this group?
Director	No, let's give them a chance.

6 children come on dressed as mountains, if possible, of varying heights. Map of the world up on OHP/whiteboard, or a large poster. As each mountain talks, another child sticks a label to the map.

Mt Everest	We are the six highest summits in the world. I am Mount Everest. I'm 8 848m high. I can be found on the border between Tibet and Nepal in the Himalayas, in Asia.
Aconcagua	(*Give time for label to be put on map.*) I am Aconcagua. I'm 6 962m high. I can be found in the Andes mountain range of South America.
Denali	(*Give time for label to be put on map.*) I am Denali. I'm 6 194m high. I can be found in the Yukon Range in Alaska, North America.
Mt Kilimanjaro	(*Give time for label to be put on map.*) I am Mt Kilimanjaro. I'm 5 895m high. I can be found in the East African range in Africa.
Mt Elbrus	(*Give time for label to be put on map.*) I am Mt Elbrus. I'm 5 642m high. I can be found in the Caucasus range in Russia, Europe.
Vinson Massif	(*Give time for label to be put on map.*) Finally, I am Vinson Massif and I'm 4 897m high. I can be found in the Ellsworth Mountains of Antartica.
Director	Mmmm. Some good information, but maybe we could cut a few of the mountains out to save on time.
Casting Dir	Yes, I see where you're coming from. Thank you, Mountains; we'll keep you updated. (*Mountains sit down.*)
Director	We seem to be getting somewhere. NEXT!

A scruffy-looking boy comes in, with a very bad attitude – not standing up straight and coming across as rude.

Actor 5   Alrigh'? Well, I'll get on with it then, shall I? Mountains can be found in every continent of the world and … er … oh yeah … animals and plants and stuff live on them … . Hang on, how much is this thing gonna pay me and do I get my own limo?

Director   What's your name?

Actor 5   Kevin.

Director   Well, Kevin, your attitude is awful. Please leave.

Actor 5   Whatever! Am I bovvered?! Speak to the hand. (*Leaves holding his hand up.*)

Casting Dir.   OK, well I think we've got the first couple of episodes wrapped up. How about we ava... lanch ('*have lunch*' in a French accent)?

Director   Don't you start – I've heard enough bad jokes today to last me a life-time!

Director and Casting Director open their lunch boxes and have their lunch. The two clowns come back on for one last time.

Clown 1   So, what did the small mountain say to the big mountain?

Clown 2   I don't know.

Clown 1   Hi Cliff!

Clown 2   Do you know what? I think we're getting worse at this! Come on, have you ever thought about a career in teaching?! That's supposed to be a barrel of laughs.

Lunch break over, the Director and Casting Director continue with the auditions.

Child walks on dressed as a snow leopard; this could be a simple label or a more elaborate costume.

Snow Leopard   Hi. I'm Leo. Now, I know what you're thinking – you're thinking, what's a nice guy like me doing so far away from home?

Director   (*Turning to Casting Director*) Well, he couldn't be more wrong!

Snow Leopard   Well, times are tough, there's not much in the way of food at the moment and I saw the ad for your programme and thought, why not?

© Katie Harris and Amanda MacNaughton

Casting Dir   (*Turning to Director*) This could be good, getting the information across from an animal's perspective. Slightly unbelievable, but would certainly add to viewer ratings.

Snow Leopard   My home is the Himalayas. Customs was a nightmare, as you can imagine! I want to tell you about what it's like living on a mountain, so I brought along some willing helpers.

4 children dressed as mountain goats walk in, shivering with fright and anxious to do and say the right thing, just in case they're eaten.

Goat 1   Bleet! I'm very grateful to be here and want to thank Leo first of all.

Goat 2   So would I. Well, where shall I start? A mountain can be a harsh environment to live in. The higher up the mountain, the cooler and thinner the air is – not a lot of oxygen.

Goat 3   This makes it quite hard for plants to survive. That's why you often find shrubs near the base of a mountain (*points to a diagram showing basic 'zones' of a mountain*).

Goat 4   In many cases, there is a 'forest zone' where alpine trees survive. Above that there is mainly grass with very few trees.

Snow Leopard   OK, now for the interesting bit. The animals. There are plenty of different types of animals that live on mountains, from the handsome yet rare snow leopard ... to the common yet most-needed (*licks his lips*) mountain goat. We manage to survive the harsh conditions by being perfectly suited to the environment. Goats, you can explain this.

Goat 1   Certainly. Well, we have thick fur to keep us warm and we are great at clambering QUICKLY (*looks nervously at leopard*) over the rocks.

Snow Leopard   I also have thick fur to keep me warm, and even the bottom of my paws have fur on them. I'm also a master at leaping from rock to rock in order to catch my prey (*glances at the mountain goats with a smile*).

Director   Thanks, that was great. We will need ALL of you to take part in the project (*looks at leopard and mountain goats*).

Goats breathe a sigh of relief and they all go and sit down.

Casting Dir   I think we're almost there. Let's get Actors 3 and 4 back for a second reading and then I think that will be it.

© Katie Harris and Amanda MacNaughton   **Brilliant Publications**   55

Director   I agree. Actors 3 and 4, please!

Actors 3 and 4 walk on and the Director gives them a script to read through.

Actor 3   Right. Shall I read from here? (*Looks at Casting Director and he/she nods back.*) 10% of the people on Earth live in mountainous environments.

Actor 4   Because of their natural beauty and range of activities, these areas attract many tourists each year. People go to places like the Alps and the Canadian Rockies for the skiing, snowboarding, hiking, climbing and nature watching, and to admire the beautiful landscapes around them. This in turn brings in jobs for the local communities and helps them to thrive.

Actor 3   However, where there are tourists, there are also problems. Litter, noise pollution and damage to the land through building and excessive use are just some of the negative issues that locals have to deal with.

Actor 4   If we can be aware of these problems and learn to respect and protect the environment around us, then this will ensure that fragile environments such as mountainous areas can thrive.

Director   Excellent. Well, I think that's a wrap! (*Turns to face audience.*) Thanks to those of you who have auditioned this morning – we'll be letting you know in due course – and to those of you who have kindly been an audience member – an even bigger thank you!

© Katie Harris and Amanda MacNaughton

And Here's One I Prepared Earlier!

Subject: Drama

Area of Study: Creative writing/Children's rights/Dance/Powerpoint

Summary: The aim of this assembly is to present a lively and popular rendition of a well-known children's TV show, covering a broad range of the curriculum. Every child in the class is given the opportunity to demonstrate their learning in school in a fun and interactive way.

Timing: 25 minutes approx

Props:
● Microphones ● packets and containers labelled with the different components needed to write a story, eg suspense, descriptive words, contrasting characters ● news desk and chair ● gold envelope ● drum

Music: Blue Peter theme tune, *Cavatina/The Deer Hunter* or piece of music suited to the style of dance chosen

Background Work:
● Creative writing – displaying the different components of writing an effective story
● PSHE work on bullying/prejudice/children's rights – posters to reflect this work (Must be readable from a distance)
● Artwork – anything recent
● Dance – small group dance originating from another country, eg line dancing from America
● ICT – class-created Powerpoint presentation based upon PSHE work 'All children have the right to …'

Cast and costumes:

Part	No needed	Suggested costumes
Presenters	3	Any – eg jeans, brightly coloured shirts
Chefs	2	Aprons, chefs' hats
Story writers	3–6	Any
Newsreader	1	Smart – eg shirt, jacket and tie, or dress or blouse
Reporter	1	Any – long overcoat
Schoolchildren	8	School uniform
Dancers	Any number	Dress suited to style of dance chosen

Suggested Script – And Here's One I Prepared Earlier!

Introductory music (theme tune to Blue Peter etc) playing.

All   Good morning!

Each child   and ... welcome ... to ... today's ...
in turn   edition ... of ... '(*add your programme title here*)'
                       coming ... to ... you ... live ... from ...
                       our ... studio ... in ... (............................) ...
                       and ... for ... today ... presented ...
                       by ...

Presenter 1   (*states name*)

Presenter 2   (*states name*)

Presenter 3   (*states name*)

Presenters step forward together and remaining children sit down.

Presenter 1   And have we got some treats for you today!

Presenter 2   Yes, we certainly have. Coming up, line dancing, all the way from
                       America! (*or dance of choice*)

Presenter 3   And of course, there are all our regular slots ... the news, competition
                       results and a look at this week's art gallery – sent in by you, the viewer.

Presenter 1   But first, we venture into the kitchen, to find out what our very own
                       celebrity chefs (............................) and (............................) are cooking up today.

Chefs are standing behind the table ready with bag of ingredients and various pieces of equipment.

Chefs   Hello!

Chef 1   Today, viewers, we have an interesting selection of ingredients – not an
                       easy mixture I'd say. What do you think, (............................)?

Both chefs are pulling ingredients out, one by one.

Chef 2   Mmmm ... a packet of suspense, some time connectives, some descriptive
                       words, a decent-size hook. You know, I think we'll be able to rustle up
                       quite a winner with this little lot – yep! A good hearty fictional story is
                       definitely on the menu today!

Chef 1   Well, let's get cracking. Creating a story in 40 minutes for a SATs test is hard enough – but in 10 minutes on live TV!

The following method could be created as a shared writing task for the whole class.

Chef 2   OK. First, let's place a couple of contrasting characters in a mixing bowl and vigorously mix with an interesting setting until it has the consistency of a smooth introduction.

Chef 1   Next, carefully combine the mixture with a good hook to keep hungry readers wanting more and more of this delicious concoction. At this stage, vivid images should be permeating the mixture.

At this stage, one or two children could read examples of their own story introductions.

Chef 2   Now add some carefully selected events, descriptive vocabulary, character's feelings (can be purchased in specialist cook shops) and thoughtfully position a handful of time connectives.

Chef 1   Now whisk all these ingredients together in order to create a tasty climax to the story.

(At this point, children could read examples from the main parts of their own story writing.)

Chef 2   Throughout all stages, don't forget to keep sieving just the right amount of punctuation in, and, to ensure a better-quality result, occasionally add a sprinkling of suspense.

Chef 1   Next, pour the mixture into a good-size ending. Scrape the bowl of all the mixture to ensure that there are no loose ends – readers won't feel satisfied otherwise.

Chef 2   Finally, bake until a golden colour – all parts should have had the same attention. Now, serve to a ready and willing audience.

(Finally, children could read examples of conclusions to their own stories.)

Presenter 2   Fantastic stuff there. We now cross over to our news desk for a special report on how ALL children have the right to an equal chance.

Newsreader   Good morning! Our report today considers the needs and rights of ALL children. Just as a bigger child can bully a smaller one in school, so a bigger group of people can treat a smaller group unfairly, simply because they have a different religion, language or way of life. That dislike is called prejudice. Treating people unfairly because they are different is called discrimination. We will all dislike someone at some time. That is just natural. It only becomes prejudice when we dislike people because of things they either cannot change or should not be asked to change. Our reporter (.....................) has been finding out more.

Reporter is with group of schoolchildren standing behind him/her holding up their anti-bullying and children's rights posters.

Reporter   Yes, I'm here in the local village school of (.................) this morning, asking children their views on issues such as prejudice, bullying and children's rights. (*Turns to first child*) So (.......................), can you explain to me the poster that you're holding there?

Child 1   Well, my poster shows the things that I believe all children have the right to, for example (*reads out parts of their poster*).

Reporter   Great! And what about your poster then? (*Turning to second child.*)

Child 2   Well, we've been discussing how to deal with bullying at school, so my poster gives advice (*reads out some advice*). It also says things like (*reads out other messages the poster gives*).

Reporter   Brilliant advice there. So (.......................), why have you been learning about prejudice then? What's it got to do with you kids and maybe some of the people watching today?

Child 3   Well, we all show prejudice every time we let our dislike or fear of people make us say or do things that are unfair.

Child 4   It's when we act on our dislikes that prejudice becomes dangerous.

Child 5   When we don't let children who are different join our group in the playground.

Child 6   When we insult them or bully them or allow them to be insulted or bullied without making a fuss.

   Brilliant Publications

Child 7   People who bully and discriminate are often frightened and scared.

Child 8   It takes real courage to stand up for someone who is being discriminated against – especially if the bullies are usually our friends.

Reporter   Wow! These kids really seem to be learning valuable lessons from their work. Let's hope our viewers have learned as much from watching this report. Thank you. This is (.....................) reporting for Blue Peter and, now, back to the studio.

Newsreader   Thank you, (.................). Well, those children have shown that, although issues like these can cause problems, there are ways to help solve these problems, and it doesn't always have to be the grown-ups who give the advice.

Presenter 3   Definitely some food for thought there! And next we'll be enjoying some of the artwork that you've been sending in for our art gallery feature.

Presenter 1   Sit back and enjoy!

All children show a piece of recent artwork whilst the Cavatina (The Deer Hunter) *music plays.*

Presenter 2   A lovely collection there, don't you think? (*Presenters 1 and 3 nod in agreement*). Well, we said we had a real treat for you today, and here they are!

Line dancing music (or other choice) begins to play as dancers step forward.

Presenter 3   (*Speaking over the music.*) Yes, all the way from America, we have the Chicago Cowboy Line Dancers performing live! (*can be changed to meet chosen style of dance etc.*)

Line dancers perform dance with clapping and occasional 'yee-hahs' from other children.

Presenter 1   Wow! That was energetic – but what fun! Thanks, guys! (*waving goodbye to line dancers.*)

Presenter 2   And finally today, if you've been waiting for the results of our 'Children's Rights Competition', then now's the time to close the door, put the dog out and listen carefully!

Presenter 3   You were asked to design a presentation of beliefs for Children's Rights and here we have the winner (*pulling name out of an envelope*). And the winner is ... (*drum roll*) ...

Presenter 1 (.....................). And you're from class (......) of (.....................) School!

Presenter 2: Well, that's all for today. Let's see how (..................) from class (......) won as we say goodbye and look forward to seeing you again soon!

Presenters 1, 2 and 3 (*All together*) GOODBYE.

Blue Peter music begins to play and Powerpoint presentation is shown.

We hope that you have enjoyed the assemblies in this book. If you would like further information about our full range of educational teacher resources, please contact us for a catalogue on 01525 222292 or look at our website: www.brilliantpublications.co.uk

Below is a selection of our range.

Ziptales provides an on-line library of over 200 interactive stories in 12 different genres, which enhance learning capabilities. The categories range from comedy, mystery, animals, and adventure to myths and legends, and true tales. All the stories from each category have worksheets linked to the National Curriculum which can be downloaded from the Internet.

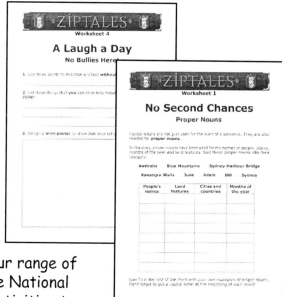

The books below represent a small selection of our range of photocopiable teacher resources. All of which are National Curriculum linked, and provide tried and tested activities to interest and stimulate children of all ages.

© Katie Harris and Amanda MacNaughton

Lightning Source UK Ltd.
Milton Keynes UK
24 November 2010

163366UK00001B/11/P